PLACER GOLD
Where to Find It

PLACER GOLD
Where to Find It

by
Gregory V. Stone

ISBN # 1-4392-3823-5
Printed in the United States of America

Fifth Printing

For more information or to order additional books, please write:

Booksurge Publishing
7290 B Investment Drive
North Charleston, SC 29418

CONTENTS

FIGURES

To my mom and dad

Introduction

The locating of a gold placer pay streak is not an easy task; if it were, we would all be rich with a minimum of effort. It is quite simple to find flour gold, but to find where the bigger nuggets and larger flakes have accumulated into a highly profitable gold placer pay streak is quite a different story.

I wrote this book because I felt that the knowledge that I had gained over the past ten years of gold prospecting would be well worth the investment that you just made in purchasing this book. I might add that I believe this book is the best little *"how-to"* gold book on the market today.

My credentials include being an instructor of a successful noncredit gold prospecting course at Eastern Montana College for the past four years, the creator and producer of the *Gold Prospector's Field Guide,* and author of *Prospecting for Lode Gold,* which has been on the market for six years.

Armed with the knowledge that is presented in this book, you may very possibly find a gold placer pay streak. I sincerely hope that you do, and when you do, please sing the praises of this work. However, gold location detection will take time and many prospecting trips, but I assure you that it will be worth the effort. I must admit that the majority of those striving to become gold prospectors lose interest within the first few months because of a lack of immediate success. For example, my first three years of prospecting were total failures. I simply didn't know what I was doing, nor did I know what prospecting actually entailed. However, I was determined to learn, and I read everything that was available on the subject of gold prospecting and made it a point to talk with knowledgeable gold prospectors and geologists. All my research on gold was presented in my book *Prospecting for Lode Gold,* which is also distributed by the same company that published the book that you are now reading. I urge you to get a copy, because it goes hand in hand with this one. My foremost desire is to have one of you find a highly profitable gold placer pay streak because of my work. I am still looking for that golden rainbow, and I hope you will beat me to the punch.

Today I can find gold traces within any stream system that traverses through a mineralized mountainous area. After reading this book you, too, will be way out in front of the other amateur prospectors, for you will know how to recognize a mineralized area that may yield gold and will know how to search out placer gold traps.

Remember that today quality placer gold sells for at least double the current selling price of bullion gold when marketed through retail jewelry outlets. Therefore, you can expect to receive higher than market quotes for bullion gold when selling placer gold wholesale to a jeweler, gold dealer, etc. There is still a lot of placer gold and lode gold left in "them thar hills" and rivers, which is verified by the fact that science estimates that 41,000 tons of gold is yet to be found in the world. This is $492 billion worth of unfound gold at $500 per ounce. Another interesting fact is that more steel is poured in one hour by industry than all the gold poured from the beginning of time. Also, I wish to inform you that probably over 80 percent of all major gold discoveries were made by amateur prospectors and not by highly trained exploration geologists working for large mining corporations.

In 1961, the United States Geological Survey predicted that perhaps ten times as many new mining districts remained to be discovered in the United States as were then known. That's one trillion dollars of mineral wealth yet to be discovered. How about getting your share?

To give you an idea of the better places to prospect, I'll go over a few more facts. Gold was first discovered in the United States in North Carolina in 1801, and the second discovery was in Georgia in 1829. How about that—these two states were the birth of the gold boom that would soon sweep the nation! The eleven top gold-producing states by rank in 1979 were Utah, South Dakota, Nevada, Arizona, Idaho, Montana, New Mexico, Colorado, Alaska, California, and Oregon. Don't discount the possibilities in the other states, because gold is where you find it. For example, much of my neighboring state of Wyoming has been scarcely prospected for gold, and I believe it has a great potential for mineral wealth.

Remember that prospecting is good for both the spirit and the body, and it will surely stir your blood. Good prospecting!

CHAPTER ONE

Chance of Finding Placer Gold

Your chance of locating placer gold today is not as good as it was in the 1800s and early 1900s, but you can find it, providing that you go about it in a scientific way. The old-timers didn't have the vast wealth of research material that is available today. We now have large geology sections within most large libraries, with multiple selections of detailed government geographical survey maps that show the complete drainage system of any creek or stream that we may wish to prospect. These contour maps show elevation rises in the landmass, enabling us to make a well-educated guess as to where we might find exposed bedrock. Today's sophisticated metal detectors now have metal settings that will detect the native metals copper, silver, gold, and platinum. We have four-wheel vehicles and thousands of miles of mountain roads that will allow access to practically any stream drainage system that we may wish to prospect. The old-timers had to follow only a handful of trails and the navigable waterways. Consequently, they flocked to areas where gold had already been discovered. Countless areas were not prospected adequately, and some areas were even overlooked because of transportation inaccessibility and the hostile conditions that existed in past eras.

We now have the tools available and the ability to discover some sizable gold finds. I am sure that there will be some good gold strikes in the coming years. All we have to do is start looking, armed with the information that is set forth in this

1

book. Also, we now have the ability to prospect remote areas—areas that were inaccessible to most of the old-timers. The old-timers perhaps got the greater share of the placer gold in the known gold fields of their day. But just think of all the areas that are yet to be prospected! If we get enough amateur prospectors out in the field searching for gold as in bygone days, new finds will definitely be made. Remember: Gold is where you find it; and this book will explain how to interpret nature's clues so that you will know how and where to find it.

CHAPTER TWO

Researching for Potential Gold Placer Areas

Before we start on a prospecting outing, we must select an area that is likely to be mineralized. To get your feet wet, I suggest starting with a known gold district within your state with proven placer deposits within its stream's system. To acquire this needed information, a trip to your city's library is an absolute must. Your library will carry the following types of research material: United States Geological Survey maps, United States Department of the Interior mining publications prepared by the staff of the Bureau of Mines, your own state's Bureau of Mines and Geology publications pertaining specifically to your state, and scores of historical mining records and old newspaper clippings that tell of your state's gold discoveries. Also, your library will usually have several good books about ghost towns that were once thriving mining camps with maps showing their exact locations. You will find countless geology books and mining books that may yield valuable information.

However, best of all research information may be purchased for a nominal fee from your state's Bureau of Mines and Geology. Write to your state's Bureau of Mines and Geology for a current list of their publications that cover the geology, mineral resources, and water resources of your state. You will be particularly interested in their geologic maps, memoirs on gold deposits, bulletins of known mining enterprises, books on geology and ore deposits, and their special publications and water resource maps. If chosen with care, these publications are extremely valuable prospecting tools, and well worth the money spent. For example, the Montana Bureau of Mines and Geology has published a list of known placer operations, and their staff has pointed out what streams they believe have the most potential for gold placer deposits. The location and production figures of commercial gold placers, when available, are given in either dollars or ounces or both. On your first prospecting trip, try a known gold production area so that you can experience the thrill of finding gold, whether it is flour gold or a small nugget. Later on you can seek your fortune in an area that is untapped.

After selecting the stream system that we wish to prospect, we must obtain a map of your state so that we may pinpoint our destination and plot a transportation route to it. In the likely event that we will have to leave the main highway and travel on dirt roads through private lands in order to reach United States Forest Service land or Bureau of Land Management (BLM) land, I suggest that you write the applicable forest service district office, requesting a forest service map of the area. These maps will show United States Forest Service access roads that pass through private land. If the land to be prospected comes under the jurisdiction of the Bureau of Land Management (BLM), their district office can provide you with maps. Forest service and BLM access roads are usually the only way to reach inaccessible United States Forest Service lands and BLM lands. All United States citizens and aliens intending to become citizens have the right to prospect on public lands under the jurisdiction of either the United States Forest Service or the BLM. However, to prospect on state lands you must obtain permission from your state's Department of Lands. On private land, permission must be obtained from the owner, with mining details and rights worked out beforehand, because mining laws do not apply. National parks and national monuments are closed to prospecting. Also, Indian lands are

4

closed to prospecting unless permission is granted from the tribal council. To obtain addresses of where to write for maps and required information, consult your telephone directory under United States Government. If a specific forest service district is not shown, call the listed district office; it can supply you with the necessary information. For BLM maps you will have to write to the nearest district office, which may not be located in your state. Your forest service people can supply you with the address of the closest district BLM office having jurisdiction of BLM lands within your state.

CHAPTER THREE

Tools Required for Gold Placer Prospecting

Now that we have selected our area within a known gold district, we will need prospector's tools. Since we will be prospecting up a gold-bearing mountain stream, a gold pan and a small sturdy shovel are absolute musts for taking gravel samples. I prefer to use a fourteen-inch, black plastic gold pan and a high-quality shovel that will not break the first time it is used. I recommend the black plastic gold pan versus the metal gold pan because you can control the materials' movement within your pan more easily because of the greater friction, or drag property, of plastic. The metal pan produces little friction, which gives you less control of the material being panned. Without the drag property, the material spills out faster, increasing your chance of losing gold. Another attribute of the black plastic gold pan is that it enables the panner to quickly spot the bright yellow gold against the black background. Other recommended equipment are a small crowbar for lifting and prying, wading boots at least waist high, rubberized gloves to protect your hands from cold water and the sharp rocks encountered when prying bedrock apart when crevicing, several spoons of various sizes for cleaning out crevices and fractures in bedrock, several glass sample bottles—7 oz. or less—for holding your gold, a wide brim hat to protect against sunburn, and a small backpack to carry the above mentioned items. These are all necessary items for gold placer prospecting.

Later on in your prospecting career you will want to acquire a four- or five-foot steel pry bar for turning over large boulders that can not be moved by one man, for working tightly wedged rocks out of crevices so that they can be cleaned out, and for prying fractured bedrock apart, giving you access to the deep-seated materials within the fracture. I guarantee that a pry bar will enable you to recover much more gold. You might object to carrying the extra weight—twenty-five to thirty pounds—but once you start using a pry bar you'll never be without one. One other item, if you are fortunate enough to own one, is a metal detector. It can be a very valuable prospecting tool for finding small nuggets or a high concentration of flour gold. The new era metal detectors, such as those made by White Electronic and other highly reputable companies, have the capability of screening out ferrous metals (those containing iron) to pinpoint the native metals copper, silver, gold, and platinum. The discrimination feature tunes out the effect of iron-bearing black sands within the river or stream gravels and detects only the gold or other native metals. However, if the gold is finely disseminated within the river gravels, it more than likely will not be detected. It certainly would detect match-size gold and larger, plus a high concentration of flour gold. I highly recommend the detector for the earnest prospector. Also, the detector would be an excellent tool for prospecting glacial moraines.

If you discover a potential gold placer, you will need a sluice box for processing more material than what you could do with a pan. The following chapter will cover panning and sluicing techniques. If you find that you have found a good pay streak, you should consider investing in a small surface dredge, preferably a three- to four-inch model to increase your production rate. I highly recommend Keene dredges. Prior to purchasing or using a dredge, check with your state's Department of Lands or Fish and Game Office to see if it can be used within your state's streams and, if so, if a permit is required. Also, your state may have set limits as to the size of the dredge that may be used.

CHAPTER FOUR

Panning and Sluicing Techniques

Now we will discuss panning techniques so that you can master the art. It is very important that you learn to pan very fast and efficiently, without losing any gold, so that you can take more gravel samples, thus increasing your gold yield. I feel that every person should develop his own method of panning. I do not describe any method as the best. However, speed, as I mentioned, is essential, and I urge all prospectors to pan quickly because you will not lose the largest nor the smallest pieces of gold once you have mastered the basics of panning. It does take practice, and I'll go through a so-called common method of panning, and I will add a teaching aid to assist you in your learning process. When you begin the learning process of panning, fill your pan with gravel and dirt. On top of this material place three to five BBs. Now submerge your pan and its material on the bottom of the stream bed, where the stream's current is slow moving, and let the water flow into and over the material in the pan (Fig. 1). Then break up the dirt lumps with your hands letting the water mix with the material. Now move the pan vigorously back and forth, from side to side, allowing a complete mixing of the stream with the material and thus letting it carry away the muddy water. As the water in the pan clears, change from a shaking, back-and-forth motion to a gentle, swirling motion, rotating your pan counterclockwise or, if you prefer, clockwise to eliminate remaining muddy water. After making sure they are

FIGURE 1—PANNING SEQUENCE

Place two to three BBs on top of your material.

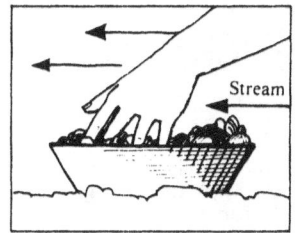

Place pan and its material on the bottom of the stream, letting the water flow over it. Mix the material with your hands, breaking up the dirt lumps.

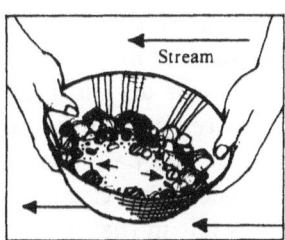

With the pan submerged under the water, shake it back and forth, from side to side, allowing the flowing stream to mix with the material and to carry away the muddy water.

Scrape off the larger rocks, and you are ready to pan.

FIGURE 1 *Continued*

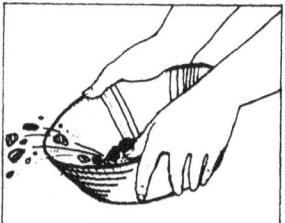 

Pan with the front lip of the pan lower than the rear lip, allowing gravity to function. Most people use a gentle, swirling motion, rotating the pan counterclockwise to eliminate remaining pebbles and muddy water.

Upon completion of panning cycle, only black sands, BBs, and gold will remain in your pan.

washed clean, scoop out the larger rocks on the top of your pan with your hands. Again shake the pan back and forth and rotate the remaining material, spilling out the lighter materials and small pebbles. As you pan, tip the pan so that the front lip of the pan (farthest from you — is an inch or more lower than the rear lip (nearest to you). Gravity will do the rest. The lighter material will spill out into the stream, and the heavier material, or concentrates, will remain in the pan. Do not tilt the pan too much or you could lose the gold. Continue this routine until only the heavy material is left in the pan. At this point, the three or five BBs that you originally placed on the top of your gravel and dirt should appear in the bottom of the pan. If you can keep the BBs in your pan, you can call yourself a qualified gold panner. Gold is approximately three times as heavy as the BBs. Therefore, you can see, it will be much easier to keep gold in your pan than it is to keep the BBs in the pan. However, I wish to warn you that the larger gold, because of its greater surface area, can get away from you faster than the smaller gold flakes and flour gold. When you pan down to the heavy material, or concentrates, begin watching for larger gold working its way up the center of your concentrates or up either side of the concentrates. If larger gold is spotted, pick it out of the concentrates with your fingers or tweezers.

Once you have located a potential gold placer or gold trap containing a pay streak, you will want to use a sluice box. It will save a great deal of time and increase your gold yield tremendously. Purchase a good one; there are many inferior ones on the market. I suggest the mini type sluice box that is approximately three feet long by ten inches wide, weighs around five pounds, and costs from thirty-five to forty dollars. The mini type is much easier to pack into remote areas than the longer, more bulky, and heavier sluice box.

The sluice box is placed in the stream parallel to the stream's flow. In other words, the stream's flow makes a right angle with the riffles of the sluice box (Fig. 2). You will need a good strong flow of water over the riffles to ensure a complete breakdown of the dirt, clay, and gravel material being dumped into the sluice box hopper. If there are two people working together, it is best to have one person shovel in the material and the other person break up the material with his hands to ensure a complete breakdown of the material and clays. Much of your gold will be embedded in clays, and the clays must be broken down to release the enclosed gold.

The best method I have come up with for controlling the water flow over the riffles is to set the sluice in a fast-moving area of the stream with the hopper, or front (water intake), of the sluice elevated slightly higher than the rear of the sluice (water outlet) to ensure greater clearing action by both water flow and gravity. To hold the sluice stationary in the stream, I place large rocks against the edge to make it immovable. To control the flow of water coming through the sluice, I place large rocks in front of the hopper to restrict the water flow. You want a good flow of water to ensure complete material breakdown and a continual discharge of gravels out of the

FIGURE 2—SLUICING SEQUENCE

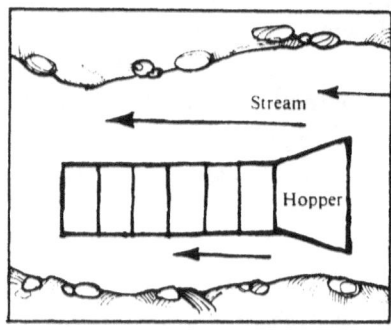

Place the sluice box parallel to the stream's flow.

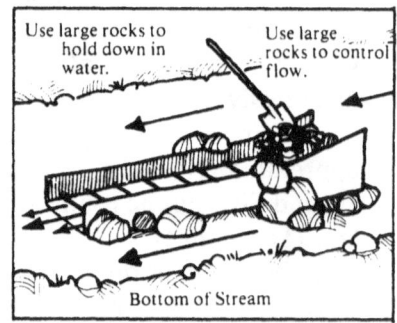

You will need a strong water flow over the riffles to ensure a complete breakdown of material placed in the hopper.

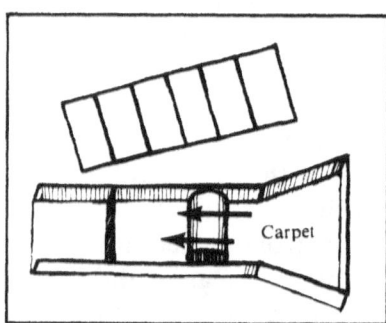

Clean up—remove riffles, and scrape the larger concentrates into your pan. Then roll the carpet and place in a pail of water.

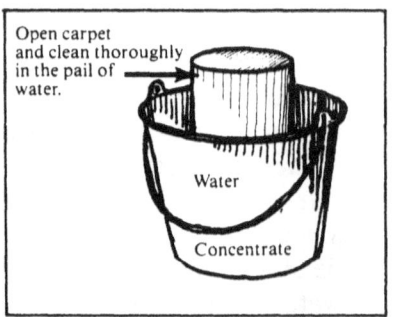

The concentrates will drop to the bottom of the pail. Now place the concentrates into your pan.

sluice box. When you have larger rocks that cannot pass through the sluice, remove them by hand so that they do not impede the flow of water. The released gold within the dirt, clay, and gravels will accumulate behind the first two riffles, with the fine flour gold dropping out farther down the sluice box. You may run your sluice for hours if you wish; but if you are like me, you will want to check it periodically. Every once in a while let the water flow without shoveling in additional gravel so that the muddy water clears and you can inspect the bottom of the sluice for larger gold. The gold that is visible and not imbedded in the carpet's mat can be removed with tweezers. To clean your sluice box, remove it gently from the stream and place it on the stream's bank, being careful not to spill out any of the contained concentrates. Then remove your riffles and again inspect for larger gold. If you find any, pick them out with your tweezers. The smaller gold will be held within the carpet and will not be visible. Scrape the larger gravels and material lying on top of the carpet with your hands cupped and place them directly into your gold pan. Now roll the carpet, again being very careful not to spill the concentrates within and lying upon the carpet. Place the rolled carpet into a pail full of water. Open the carpet in the pail and wash out all the trapped concentrates into the water. Once cleaned, the carpet can be placed back in the sluice box and the riffles snapped back into place over the carpet.

We are now ready to pan our concentrates using our own panning method. Since we have already loaded our pan with the larger-sized concentrates from the sluice, we will start with it. When you are panning concentrates from a sluice, you must pan slower than usual. This is because now you have an abnormally high concentration of potential gold-bearing concentrates, which you don't have when you pan a single pan of stream gravel. Therefore be a little slower, just to make sure you don't lose any of the gold. Next take the concentrates from the bucket and place them into your pan and again pan very carefully.

13

As I stated before, gold has a specific gravity of 15 to 19 and will definitely stay in your pan. After you have completed your panning you will find only black sand and gold. The gold will first appear at the outer edge of the black sand. When first learning to pan, many people are confused by pyrites and weathered mica. However, this confusion ends quickly after you have found gold in two or three pans of gravel. The best way to know if the metallic shine that you see is gold or pyrites and weathered mica is to shade your hand over the suspected gold. Without sunlight's reflective properties, you will not be able to see the pyrites and mica; but if it is gold, you can still see its yellow color. Another test is to take the material that looks like gold from the pan and place it between your teeth. Gold will not crumble when you bite down, it is malleable and will show the indentation of your tooth. If it is fool's gold, pyrite, it will not indent when you bite down. Don't bite down with a lot of pressure because you could break a tooth. Pyrite (iron sulphide) is usually cube shaped, pale brassy yellow, and has a metallic luster. Its physical appearance is nothing like gold. Placer gold does not have cleavage; it takes on almost any conceivable shape. It looks like molten metal or a drop of solder. Gold can range in color from silvery yellow to yellow and silver white to orange red when impure. I might add that placer gold is normally around 97 percent pure. Weathered mica also fools some amateur prospectors because it looks like flakes of gold, but it will crumble when bitten, or when squeezed between your fingers. Nitric acid can also be used for testing suspected gold because both iron pyrites and mica are soluble in it, whereas gold is not affected. Once you have encountered the real thing—gold—in your pan, you'll never mistake anything else for it.

To remove the small flour gold and small flakes from your pan, rotate a small amount of water through the black sand, moving them away from the heavier gold. If you have large flakes, you can push them out from the black sand with your fingertip. Now I'll go over my procedure for getting the gold out of the pan and into a water-filled sample bottle. I find that if I lick the top of my finger and then touch my finger to the gold, it will adhere to my finger. I can move the gold to the bottle, and it will not come off my finger until it makes contact with the water in the bottle.

When I get home from my prospecting trip, I pour most of the water from the sample bottle into the kitchen sink, leaving approximately a fourth of the water in the bottle. I then place my thumb over the neck of the bottle and turn it upside down, bringing the remaining water, gold, and black sand against my thumb. I then release my thumb, dropping the gold, remaining water, and black sand onto an absorbent paper towel. I let it dry thoroughly, usually overnight. Then I take a white piece of typing paper and press it firmly against the towel and invert their positions very quickly. This places the gold on the typing paper. Now you have just your gold and some grains of black sand on the typing paper. To remove the black sand, just blow with your mouth. The sand will blow away and leave just the gold. Make a crease in the typing paper and pour the gold into a clean sample bottle that has no water in it. That's all there is to it. It's the quick and simple method that I have come up with.

Recognition of a Mineralized Area

Before we get into gold placers, we should know how to recognize a mountainous area that is mineralized. First we must learn how to discriminate among young mountains (Fig. 3), mature mountains (Fig. 4), and old mountains (Fig. 5). Young mountains are very rugged, with steep slopes, barren cliffs, and high sharp-pointed peaks. You find very little erosion in young mountains, which is evident by the lack of talus, or rock debris, lying at the base of their cliffs. You will be wasting your time prospecting in young mountains, because there has been a minimum amount of erosion and there have been no subsequent upheavals, intrusions of magma, that bring the deep-seated ore deposits to the surface. In young mountains, the deep-seated ore deposits can only be detected with highly sophisticated metal detecting and homing devices that are carried aboard exploration-rigged aircraft. Once a detection is made from the air of a potential ore deposit, its value can only be proved by extensive core drilling within that designated area. As you can see, only large mining companies could finance such an expensive exploration program.

Therefore, we will be most interested in the mature mountains that show much faulting. Within the mature mountains there has been subsequent intrusions that have brought the once deep-seated ore deposits to the surface, where erosion has exposed the mineralized outcrops. The intrusion will also create new ore deposits. Mature mountains that contain

FIGURE 3—YOUNG MOUNTAINS

They are identifiable by their ruggedness, sharp peaks, and lack of erosion. Here ore deposits are deep-seated and can be found only by the use of expensive metal-detecting equipment and extensive core drilling. Erosion or subsequent upheavals have not brought ore deposits to the surface.

FIGURE 4—MATURE MOUNTAINS

They are less rugged than young mountains, erosion is much greater, and their peaks are more rounded. Faulting is more prominent, indicating subsequent upheavals because of intrusive activity. These mountains contain ore deposits nearer the surface.

FIGURE 5—OLD MOUNTAINS

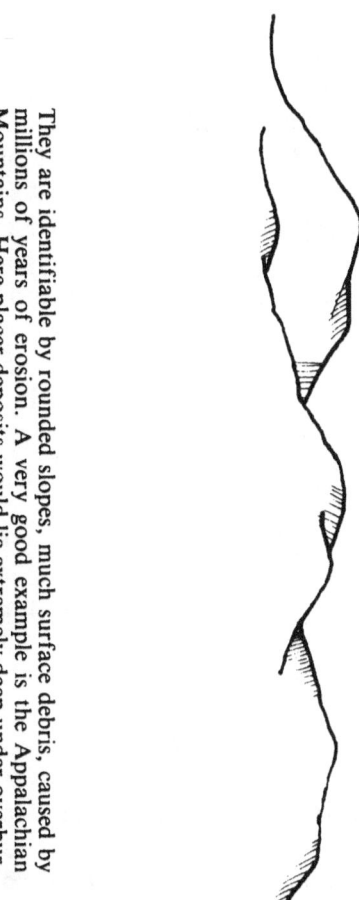

They are identifiable by rounded slopes, much surface debris, caused by millions of years of erosion. A very good example is the Appalachian Mountains. Here placer deposits would lie extremely deep under overburden.

faults, folds, and volcanos are called complex mountains. Complex mountains (Fig. 6), are a combination of faulted mountains (Fig. 7), folded mountains (Fig. 8), and volcanic mountains (Fig. 9). Faults, folds, and volcanos result when an igneous intrusion and/or deep-seated magma is intruded, or literally pushed up into the older existing landmass or existing mountains. The result is a complex mountain range such as the Rocky Mountains. The mature mountains are easily distinguishable from young mountains because their slopes are more gentle, large talus deposits lie beneath their cliffs, and there are no or very few sharp-pointed peaks. I might add that whenever you see large talus deposits within a mountainous area it indicates mineralization. Mineralized rocks will decompose much more rapidly than rocks containing little or no mineralization. As you can see, the prospector is most interested in the complex mountains/mature mountains because they hold the greatest potential for mineralization that may host gold deposits.

The third class of mountains are the old mountains that have been weathered down to gentle slopes with rounded tops and few jagged border features. A very good example of an older mountain range is the Appalachian Mountains. In old mountains, we find deep erosion that would leave any gold placer deposits buried deep under vast amounts of eroded overburden, rocks and dirt, that have weathered from the mountains and accumulated over millions of years. These mountains would be relatively unimportant to the prospector.

Since I have mentioned an igneous intrusion or subsequent upheaval several times within this chapter, I will explain how it creates a complex mountain range (Fig. 6). Complex mountains are where the prospector is most likely to find both placer and lode gold. First, I will mention the batholith, which is the largest type of igneous intrusive body. It is formed from the plutonic, or very deep, rocks, which are believed to have formed near the boundary between the mantle rock and the earth's crust. Plutonic rocks are molten rocks of stupendous

FIGURE 6—COMPLEX MOUNTAINS

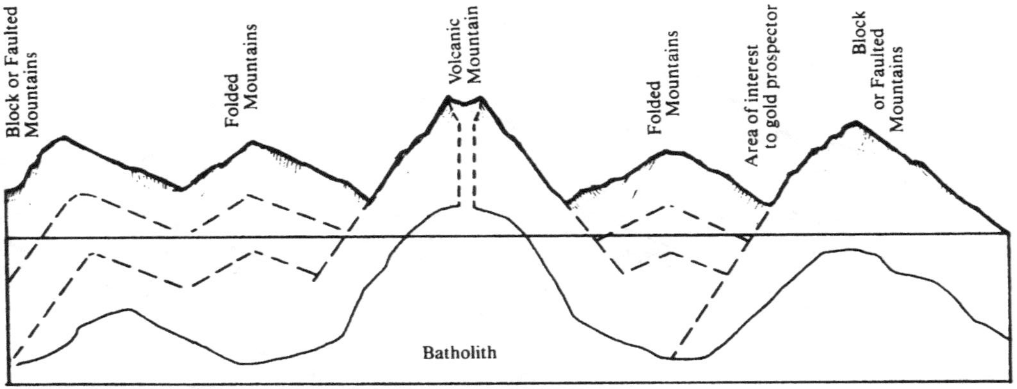

Block or Faulted
Mountains

Folded
Mountains

Batholith

Volcanic
Mountain

Folded
Mountains

Area of interest
to gold prospector

Block
or Faulted
Mountains

These mountains show folding, faulting and volcanic activity caused by igneous intrusions. A good example of complex mountains are the Rocky Mountains of the western United States. Complex mountains are very important to the gold prospector.

21

FIGURE 7—FAULTED MOUNTAINS

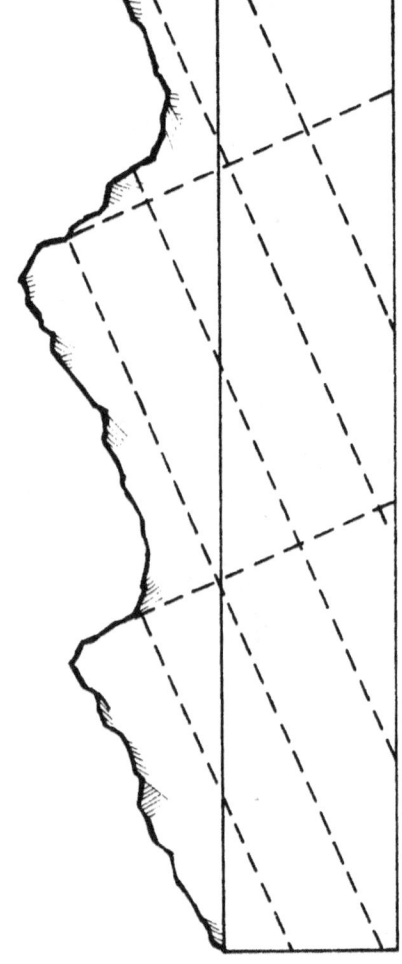

Faulted mountains usually have a short, steep slope on one side and a long, gentle slope on the other side. Faulted mountains are very important to the prospector. Faults create veins and fissures that may be highly mineralized.

FIGURE 8—FOLDED MOUNTAINS

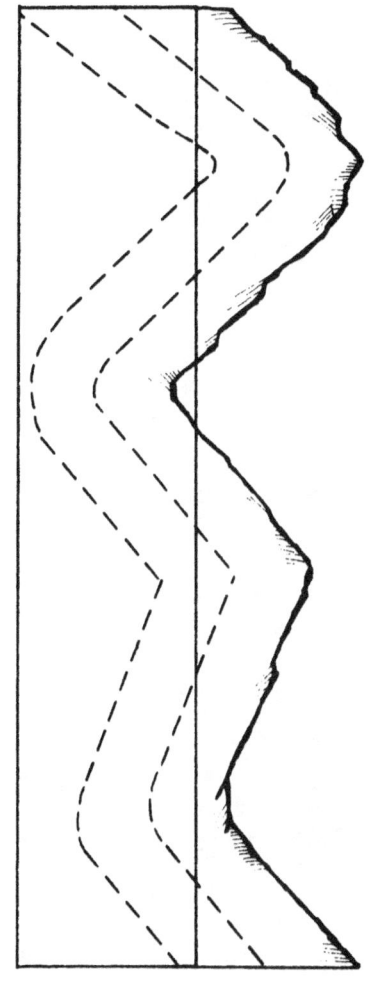

Folded mountains are a result of intrusive activity and are usually accompanied by faulting. The Rocky Mountains are also folded mountains. Folded mountains are of importance to the gold prospector.

FIGURE 9—VOLCANIC MOUNTAINS

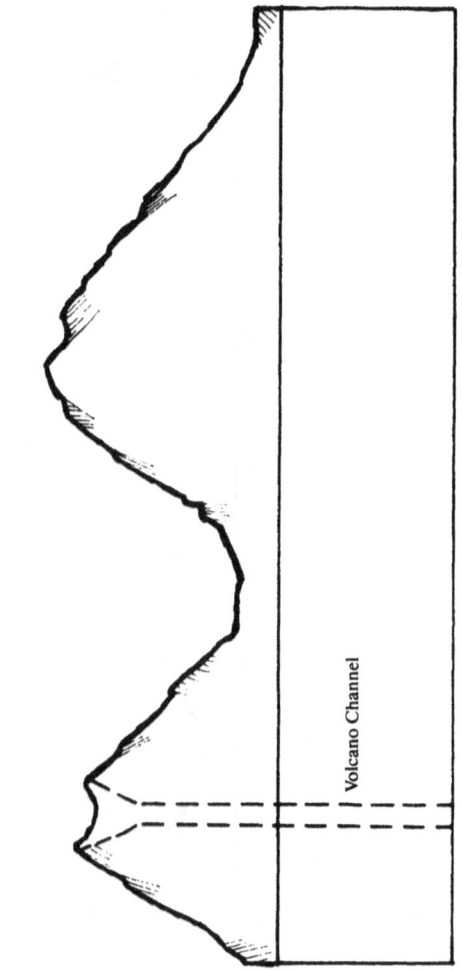

Volcano Channel

Volcanic mountains are mountains which have been created by extrusive igneous activity. They are of little importance to the gold prospector and have few commercial deposits.

size. Large mountain chains, such as the Rockies, are but mere bulges of the larger plutonic masses underneath. From them appear the batholith, a bulging upward extension of the plutonic material underneath known as the magma, which has pushed its way toward the surface by buckling and melting rocks above it. In doing so, the magma, or batholith intrusion, creates faulting, folding, and volcanic activity which in turn produces a complex mountain range. The magma has literally pushed its way into the host, or intruded, existing rock or mountain by force and, in doing so, has induced the development of outer border features such as joints, fissures, dikes, and veins that are mineralized during the cooling-off period of the magmatic intrusion. Hydrothermal solutions are given off in the late stages of magmatic cooling, and they flow through openings such as faults, fissures, veins, and porous rocks, seeking areas of lower pressure. These hot waters carry vast quantities of mineral and ore matter in solution, which create the ore deposits within complex mountains. Also, as I mentioned before, the upheaval will bring existing deep-seated ore deposits within the intruded mountains nearer to the surface. For additional information on how mineralization occurs, please obtain a copy of my book *Prospecting for Lode Gold*.

A mineralized area can also be determined by the rocks and minerals that you find in your gold pan, and the method by which to do that will be discussed in the following chapter.

CHAPTER SIX

Gold Placer Deposits

Before we begin our prospecting trek up a known gold-bearing stream, I'll explain and diagram the geological process involved in the creation of a gold placer pay streak. Gold placer deposits are the result of decomposed and eroded mineral and metal-bearing rocks, lode gold, being carried by water and glacier from higher hills and mountains. The gold materials they contain are deposited into basins, faults, creeks, and rivers (Fig. 10). Gold placers are usually found in stream and river beds (Fig. 11). Because most streams and rivers travel many miles, we must learn to spot potential gold traps within the stream's system or we will waste many valuable hours in futile prospecting. In other words, we will need to locate areas within the stream's system where bedrock is either exposed or is very close to the surface and can be easily dug down to. Bedrock is the solid rock underlying the overburden of a stream. Overburden is the boulders, rocks, gravels, dirt, and clays that lie over the stream's bedrock. Gold is usually found lying on the bedrock or within a foot or two above it. If you cannot find bedrock or dig down to it easily, you will be wasting your time. The average depth of overburden within a stream's system is approximately fifteen feet. In some areas of the stream it can be forty feet or more. As you can readily see, without expensive equipment, such as bulldozers and backhoes, it is impossible to work suspected gold deposits lying beneath many feet of overburden.

26

FIGURE 10—GOLD PLACER DEPOSIT

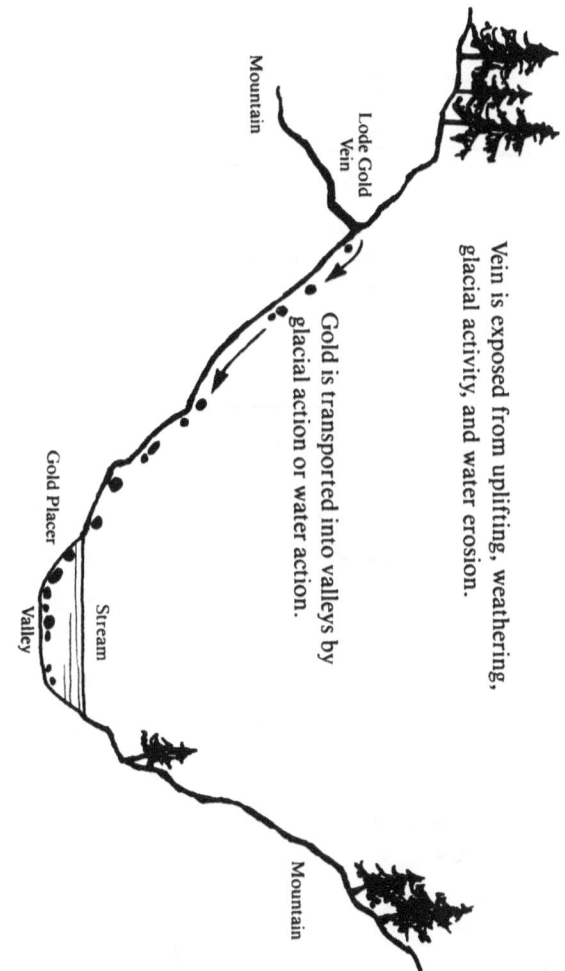

Mountain

Lode Gold
Vein

Vein is exposed from uplifting, weathering,
glacial activity, and water erosion.

Gold is transported into valleys by
glacial action or water action.

Gold Placer

Stream

Valley

Mountain

27

FIGURE 11—STREAM OR
ALLUVIAL PLACER FORMATION

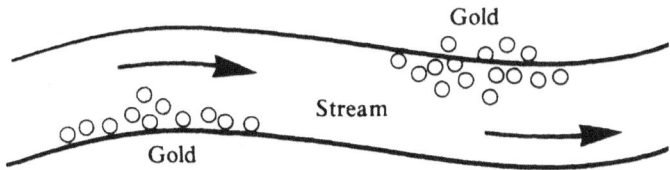

In a rapidly flowing, meandering stream, the fastest water is on
the outside curve of meanders and slow water on the inside curve.
The junction of fast and slow water, where gravel beds form, is the
area of gold deposition.

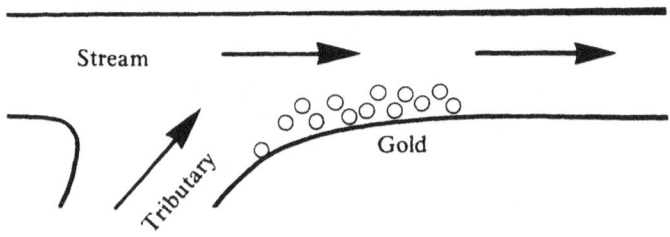

Where minerals and gravels are transported by a swift tributary
into a slower-flowing stream, the gold accumulates at the near
side.

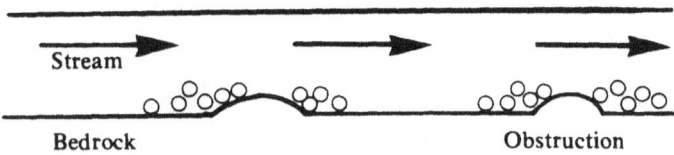

Where streams cross highly inclined rocks, the gold is caught, as in
the riffles in a sluice box.

As we travel up a stream's drainage system, we must search for land features (Fig. 12, 13, 14, 15, 16) that are clues for finding exposed bedrock that may have gold traps within that immediate area. Now that you have taken some time to study these land feature diagrams, I'll explain a simple technique that can be used for locating these land features, other than by walking up the stream and visually seeing them, with the aid of a United States Geological Survey contour map. Obtain a contour map of the area that you wish to prospect from the United States Geological Survey, Denver, Colorado 80225, or from your hometown public library. Most survey stores will carry a good selection of contour maps that are applicable to your state.

I have drawn a sample contour map (Fig. 17) that shows you how to determine in what area of the stream's drainage system you would be most likely to find exposed rock outcrops that may extend down to or into the stream. The distance between the contour lines indicates the slope of the terrain. The closer the lines, the steeper the slope, which indicates the probability of land features that may contain exposed rock outcrops—such as canyons, cliffs, etc.—where you could expect to find bedrock and its gold traps.

Once in the field, we will search for land features such as cliffs, canyons, and exposed rock outcrops that come close to the stream's edge, and we will be especially interested in those outcrops that actually jut out into the stream. Here you will normally find exposed bedrock in the stream, or you will be able to reach it with a minimum amount of shoveling. After exposing the bedrock , we hope to find gold traps within it and perhaps a gold pay streak. Before we continue, I wish to stress that when you walk up a stream, always be sure to look for exposed bedrock within the stream's bed, even though the abovementioned land features are not present. Sometimes you will find an exposed section of bedrock in relatively flat terrain with no rock outcrops jutting out from the stream. Here we have exposed bedrock that was perhaps elevated because of

FIGURE 12—GOLD TRAP

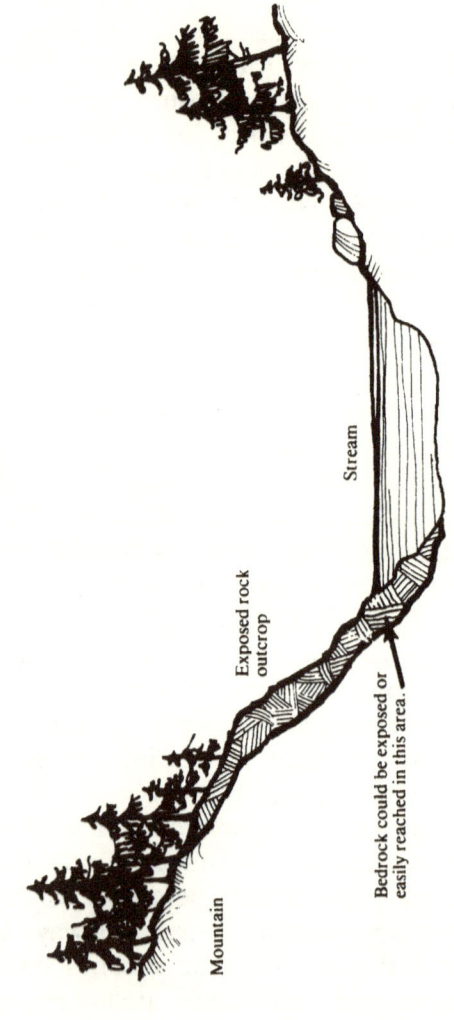

Mountain

Exposed rock outcrop

Stream

Bedrock could be exposed or easily reached in this area.

30

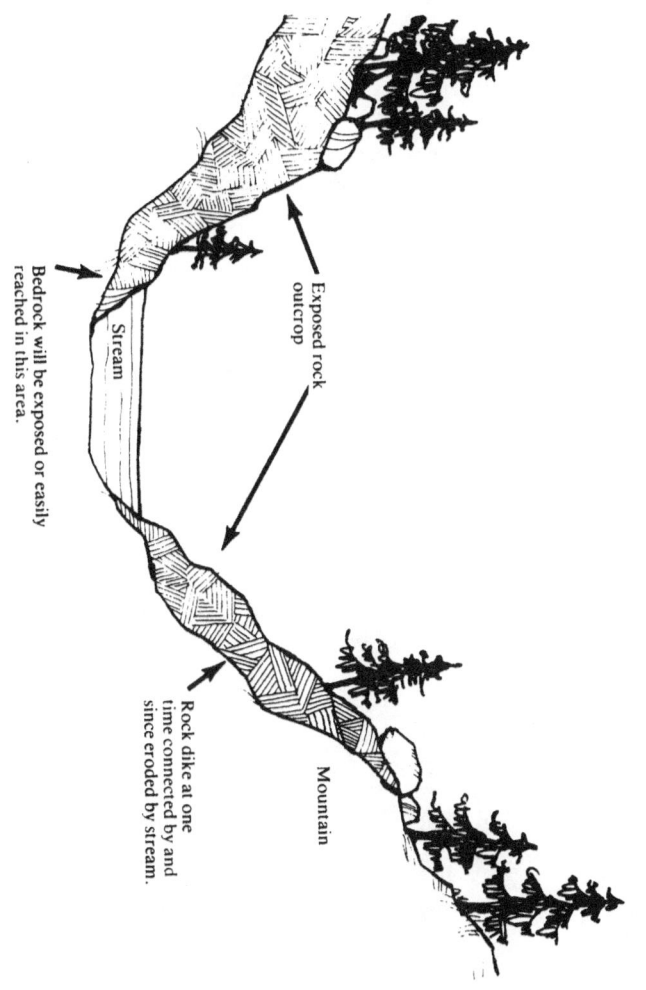

FIGURE 13—GOLD TRAP

Exposed rock outcrop

Bedrock will be exposed or easily reached in this area.

Stream

Rock dike at one time connected by and since eroded by stream.

Mountain

31

FIGURE 14—GOLD TRAP

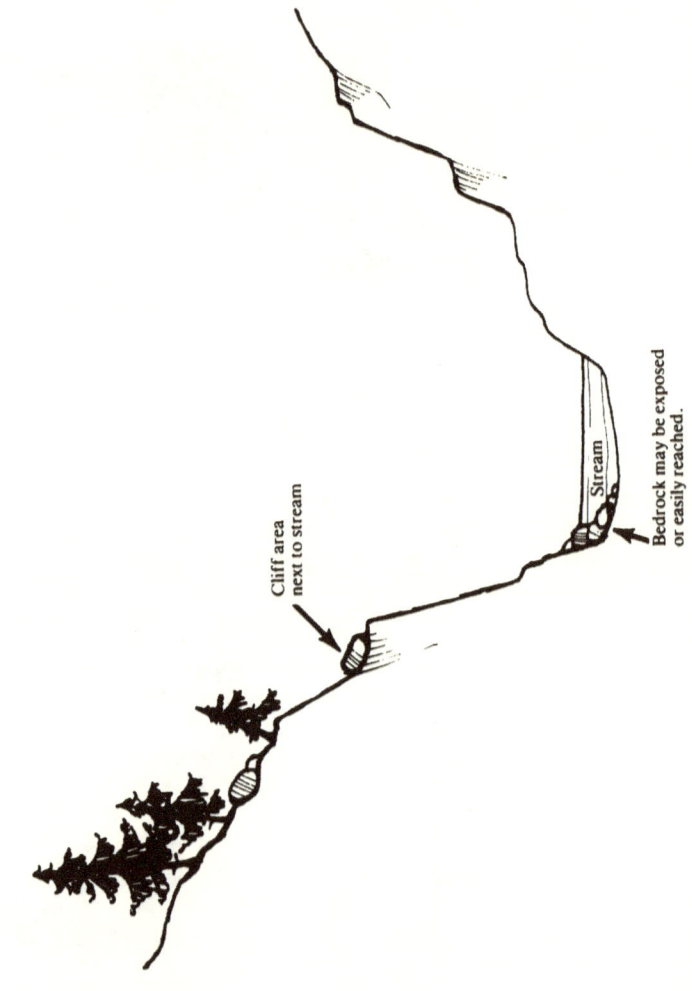

Cliff area
next to stream

Stream

Bedrock may be exposed
or easily reached.

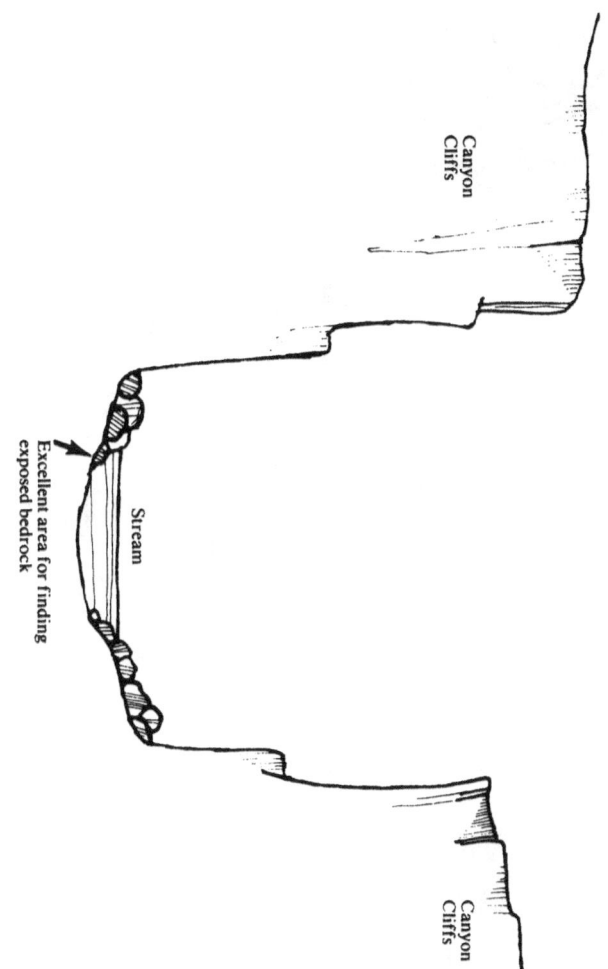

FIGURE 15—GOLD TRAP

33

FIGURE 16—GOLD TRAP

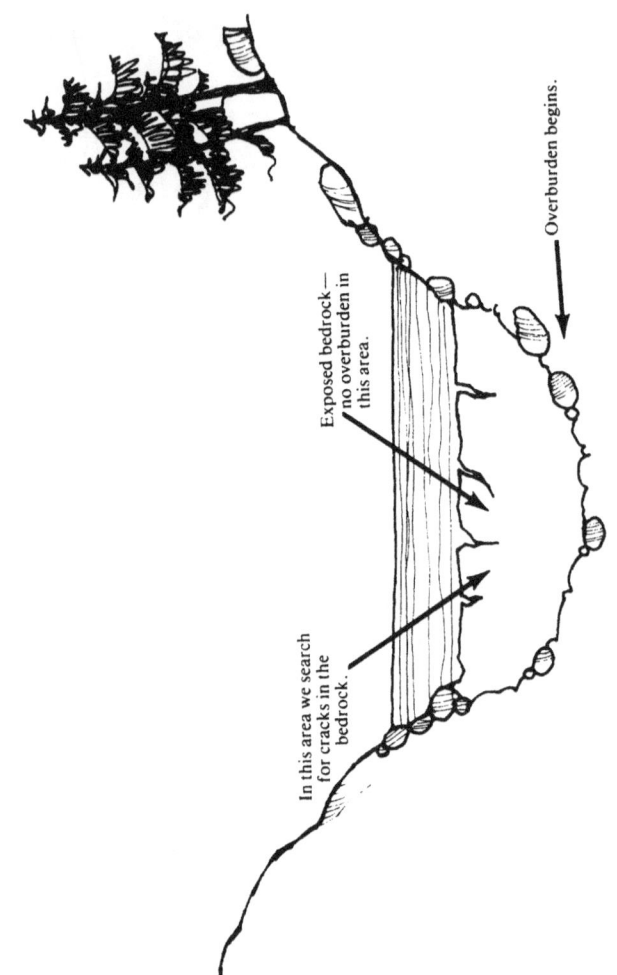

In this area we search for cracks in the bedrock.

Exposed bedrock — no overburden in this area.

Overburden begins.

34

FIGURE 17—CONTOUR MAP

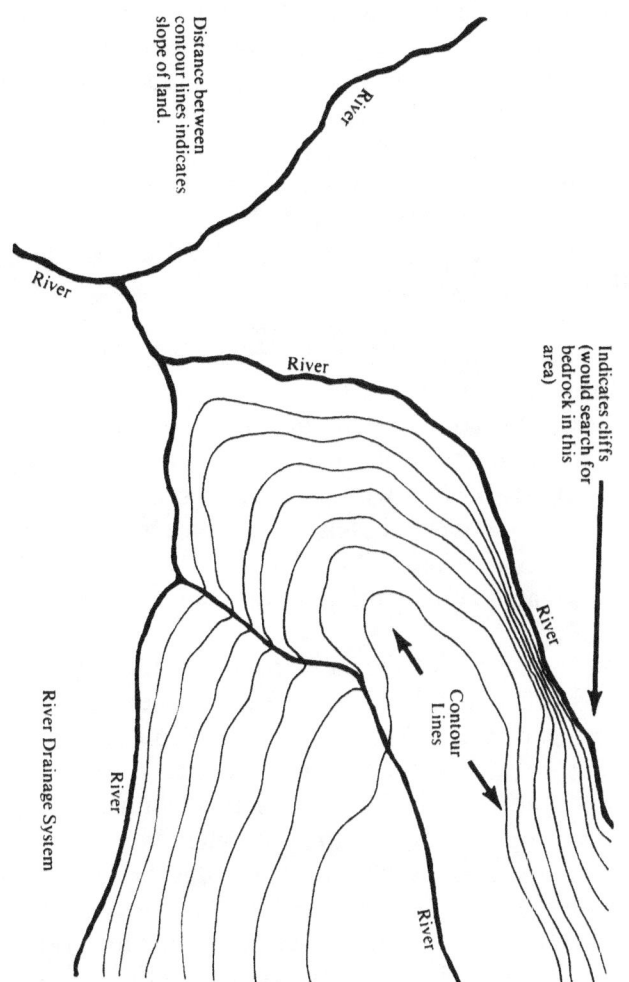

Distance between contour lines indicates slope of land.

Indicates cliffs (would search for bedrock in this area)

Contour Lines

River Drainage System

River

River

River

River

River

River

35

folding, creating an anticline (an arch of stratified rock) that has been exposed from stream action (Fig. 18).

Once we have located an area with exposed bedrock, we will use an excellent gold-prospecting technique to determine whether there is gold in the area. The technique is called *mossing*. However, before I describe the mossing technique to you, I will explain how to determine whether or not you are prospecting in a mountainous area that is mineralized and that may subsequently contain gold deposits. By taking gravel samples at various spots within the stream's bed and by sampling gravels lying away from the water's edge, you can determine if the area is mineralized. Pan the material and watch for pebbles and sand grains that are red, white, green, brown, blue, pink, transparent, or metallic in color. If you find these indicators, it shows that you are in an area of mineralization. Especially watch for milky-white quartz, because it is the gangue (host mineral) associated with all major gold deposits. If we have found only coarse gravels in our pan and no smooth, rounded gravels, we know that little erosion has taken place within the stream's system and that our chance of finding gold is very unlikely.

Now let's get back to the mossing technique, for we now know the area is mineralized because of the indicators that we have found in our pan. Mossing can be accomplished at any time, anywhere within the stream's drainage system. To save exploration time it should be performed as soon as you begin your prospecting trek up the stream. When you spot a good growth of moss either at the stream's edge or farther away from the edge, higher on the bank, take the moss sample and with it scrape the fine dirt underneath the moss into your gold pan. Now take the collected moss sample and dirt to an area of the stream where the current is slow and submerge your pan into the stream. Break up the moss with your hands, releasing the fine material that is held within it. Pan the material, using the same panning method discussed in Chapter Four. You should find black sand (magnetite) and very fine flour gold

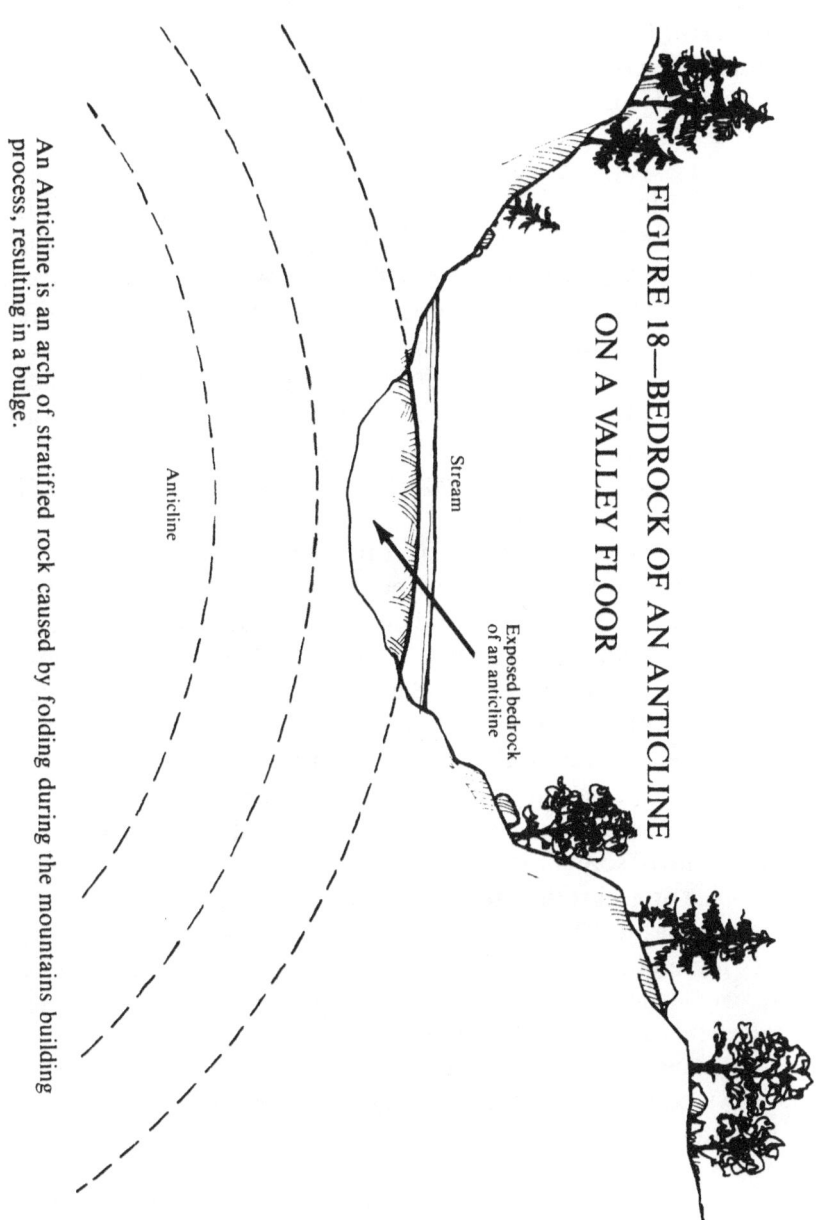

FIGURE 18—BEDROCK OF AN ANTICLINE ON A VALLEY FLOOR

Stream

Exposed bedrock
of an anticline

Anticline

An Anticline is an arch of stratified rock caused by folding during the mountains building process, resulting in a bulge.

approximately the size of a pin tip, provided there is gold in the area. However, so that you do not err in the mossing technique, I recommend that you accomplish the moss test several times, selecting moss samples from various elevations along the stream's bank and at several locations within the stream's system as you prospect up it. You will find flour gold normally at the spring runoff level of the stream bed. The spring runoff level is the highest level that a stream will reach during the year. I have mentioned this before but wish to reiterate this very important point: Please don't confuse a stream's bed with bedrock. The stream's bed is the current channel that lies over the overburden and over which the stream flows (Fig. 19). The bedrock lies beneath the overburden and is the absolute bottom, or solid rock, that is eventually encountered when you remove the overburden (boulders, rocks, gravels, dirt, and clays) that lie above it.

At this time I wish to go over the placer gold clues, or indicators, that we will hope to find in our gold pan. I will cover the six mineral and rock gold clues and will then place special emphasis upon the two most important clues that are almost always found within a gold placer deposit. The six gold placer clues are: black sand (magnetite), an iron-bearing sand with a high specific gravity that is usually associated with gold and will line your pan upon completion of the panning cycle; garnet, a transparent deep-red mineral that indicates mineralization and is sometimes but not always associated with gold; pebbles or grains that are red, green, brown, blue, pink, transparent, or metallic in color, which show that you are in an area of mineralization; quartz—especially milky-white colored quartz which produces the greatest share of gold and is an excellent clue that placer gold may be found; clays—rust colored clays that turn the water in your pan to an orange or rust-brown color are associated with gold placers; gold, flour gold, and gold flakes which indicate that larger gold grains and nuggets may be found upstream. It's self-evident that the best clue is actual gold, flour gold, and flake gold as they indicate that

FIGURE 19—PLACER DEPOSITS

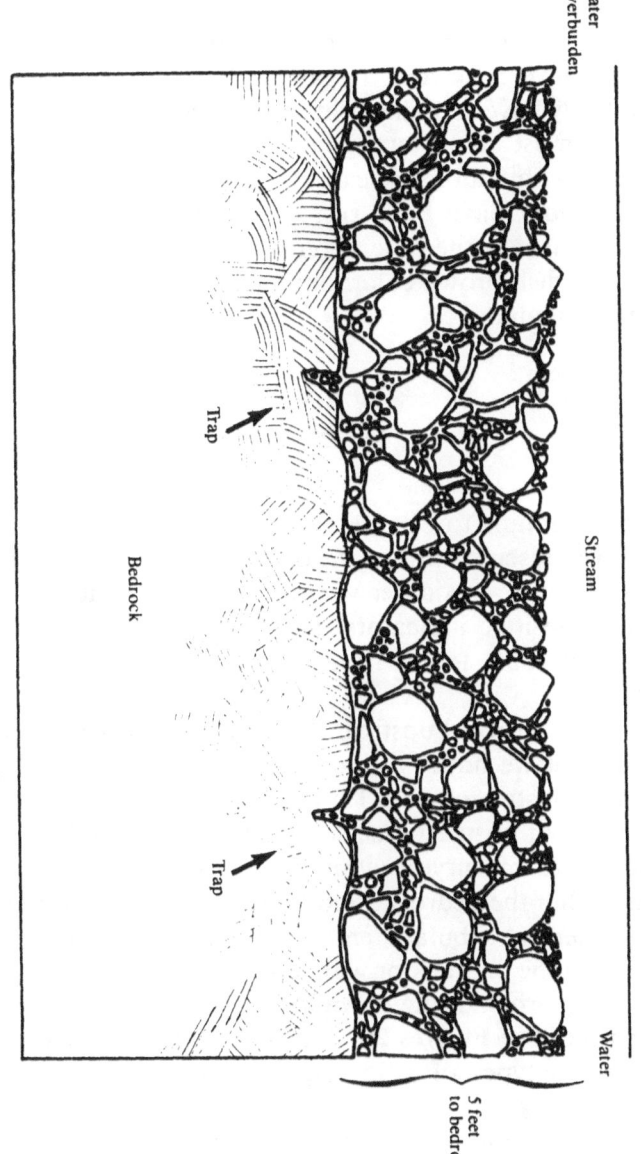

Water
Overburden

Stream

Water

Trap

Trap

Bedrock

5 feet
to bedrock

Gold usually lies on bedrock or within two feet of it.

we may find a gold placer pay streak upstream with larger grains and nuggets. However, flour gold does not necessarily mean that there is larger gold or nuggets farther upstream, because the host rock and its gangue from which the gold came may only have contained fine flour gold.

The two most important gold placer clues that I have encountered within all the stream systems where I have recovered placer gold have been rust- or reddish-brown-colored clays, which have turned the water within my gold pan to an orange or reddish-brown color; and black sand, which is usually found in abundance.

AU

Before continuing to Chapter Seven on assaying a potential placer, we will discuss some of the more lucrative kinds of gold traps that we may encounter while prospecting. Thus far we have found positive indicators that we are in a mineralized area and have now found flour gold by using the mossing technique.

Now we will proceed upstream to seek the bedrock and the gold traps that we hope will be found there. Here I wish to reiterate that in streams (Fig. 11) gold will usually be found on the down side of obstructions, such as boulders and dikes; on the inside bend of curves within the stream; in potholes or fractures within the bedrock; and on the down stream side of the area where a tributary enters the stream. Gold almost always lies on the bedrock or within a foot or two of it. If you cannot find bedrock or dig down to it easily, you will be wasting your time. See Figures 20, 21, 22, and 23. These are the most common types of gold traps that you will encounter when prospecting.

Coarse gold is found more often in the deeper channel, and the fine gold is usually found in the shallow areas farther away

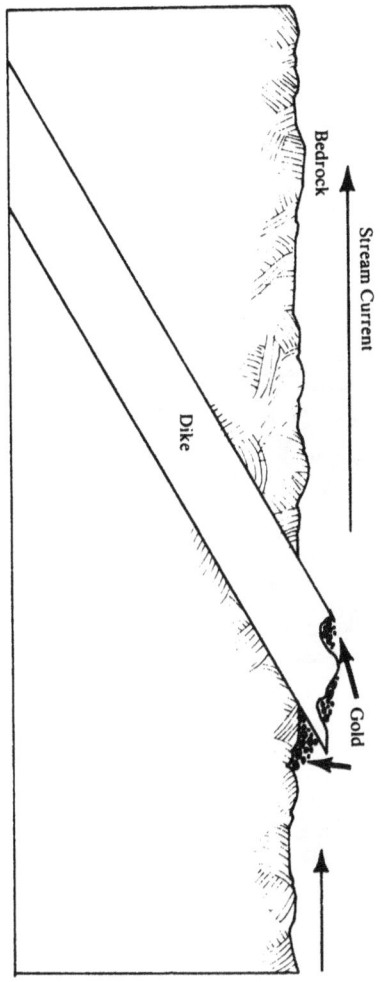

FIGURE 20

41

FIGURE 21

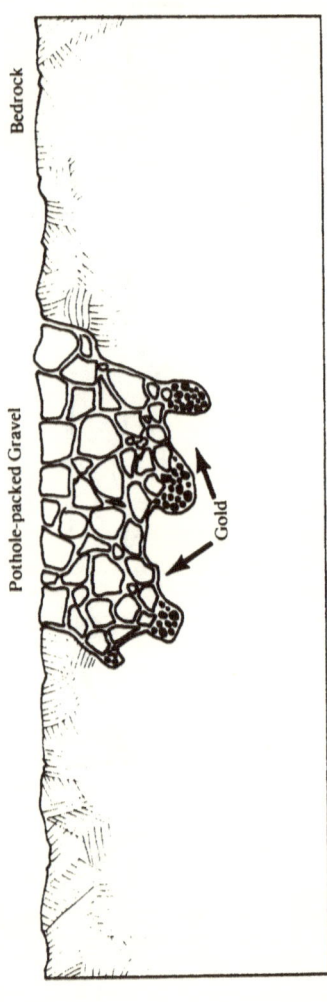

FIGURE 22—BEDROCK CREVICE STRUCTURE

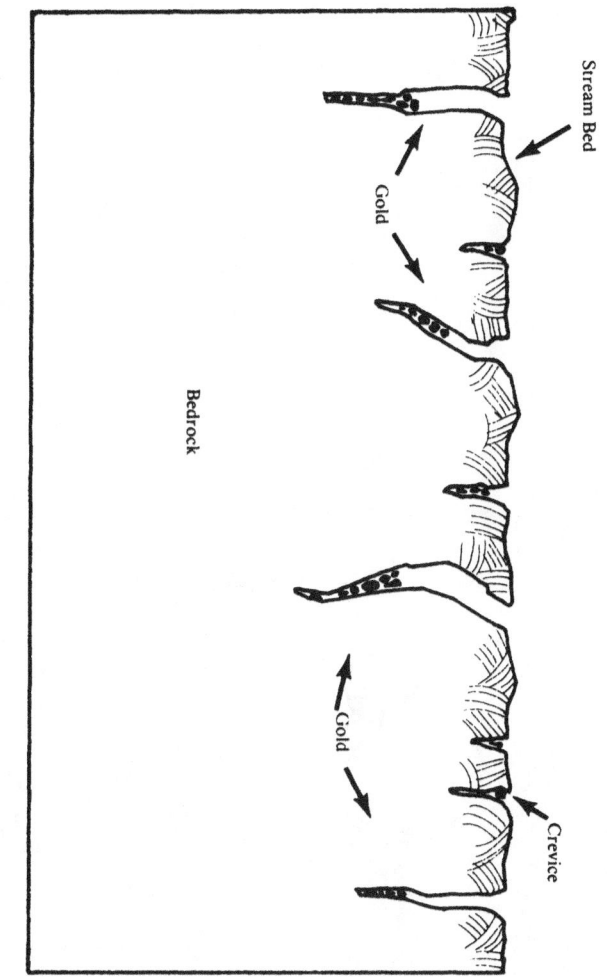

Stream Bed

Gold

Bedrock

Gold

Crevice

Gold usually lies on the bedrock, in bedrock fissures, and/or within a foot or two of the bedrock.

FIGURE 23

Looking down at stream with exposed bedrock, showing parallel and vertical fissures or cracks.

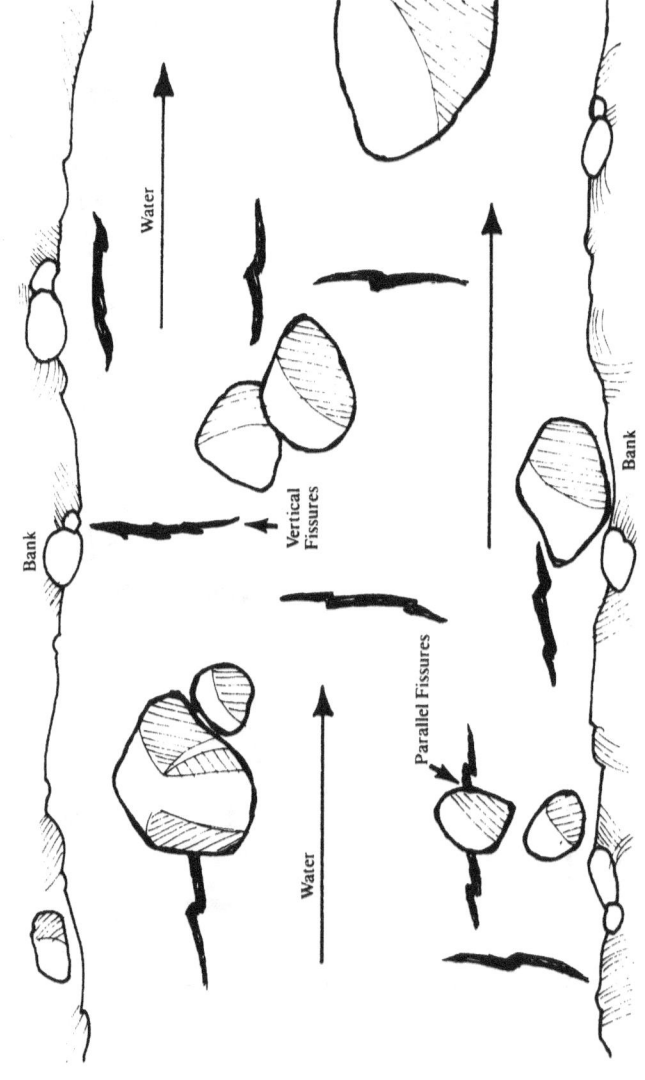

Water

Bank

Vertical Fissures

Parallel Fissures

Water

Bank

Parallel fissures and vertical fissures make excellent gold traps.

from the main stream channel. When we find fractures or a deep pothole on the bedrock's surface, we should clean out the cracks and potholes and pan the collected material. Slates and rocks that produce rock plates that jut up from the bedrock produce excellent gold traps. Gold will fall between the plates, becoming trapped until it is found (Fig. 24). If rough gold flakes or jagged nuggets with milky quartz still attached are found in our pan, we can assume that we are close to the gold's source. The angularity of gold is inversely proportional to the distance traveled. Placer gold tends to occur in concentrated pay streaks that are narrow and relatively rich. If the gold that we find is coarse, we will proceed up the stream, taking additional samples. If we find no more gold nuggets upstream, we will assume that we are in the area of the gold lode that fed the placer and will leave the stream's bed to search for it. For additional information on finding the lode, obtain a copy of my book *Prospecting for Lode Gold.*

Once we have found gold in a stream's system, whether it is flour gold or larger gold, we must constantly be searching for ancient placers. Remember that placer gold was weathered out of the host rock and its gangue (principally quartz) millions of years ago and was transported and deposited by water and glacial action. The stream bed that you are panning in now is of recent origin, and the gold that it contains most likely came from an ancient stream channel that has been uplifted or laid somewhere else within the valley's floor during a different geological time (Fig. 25, 26). The recent river channel has washed through the ancient river channel, capturing the gold within it and redepositing it within its channel. Or the uplifted placer may now lie halfway up the mountainside or maybe twenty to eighty feet above the recent channel, or perhaps it is lying on top of the mountain. In these instances the gold is washed down from the uplifted placer from melting snow runoff or is transported down into the valley by glacial action. I would guess that practically all the placer gold found today originated from ancient stream systems. The best method that I

FIGURE 24

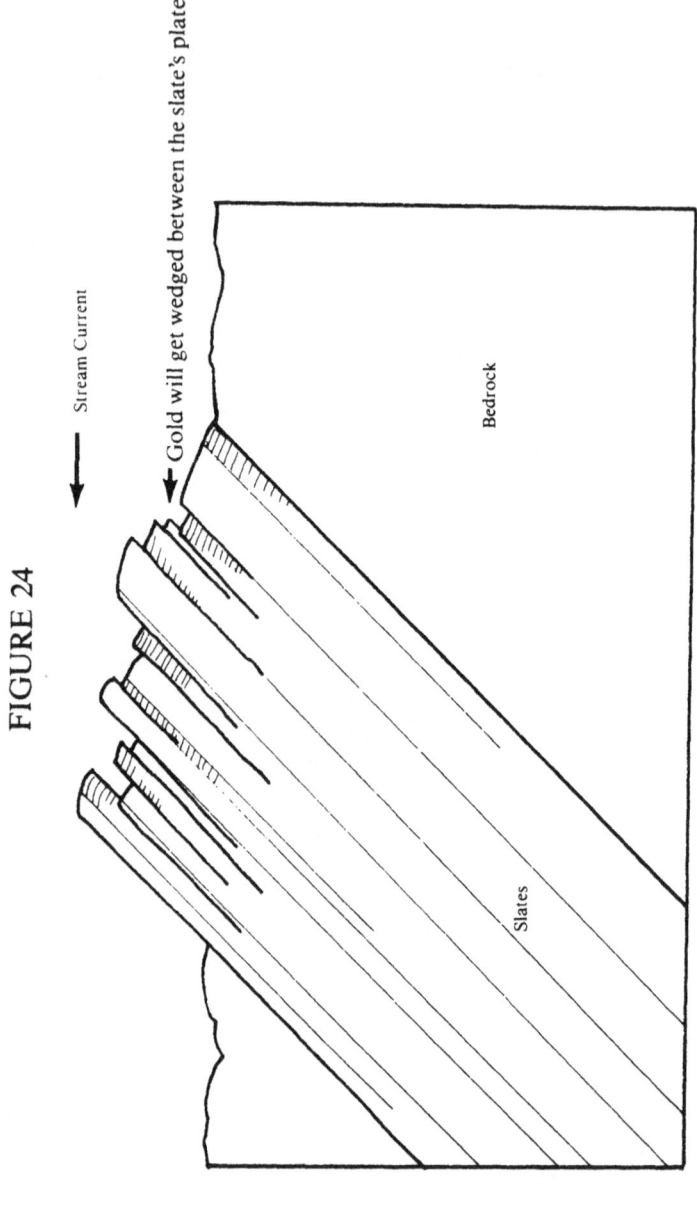

Stream Current

Gold will get wedged between the slate's plates.

Bedrock

Slates

FIGURE 25—OLD AND NEW RIVER CHANNELS INTERSECTING

A new river channel would be void of gold if it were not intersecting with an ancient river channel that did carry gold.

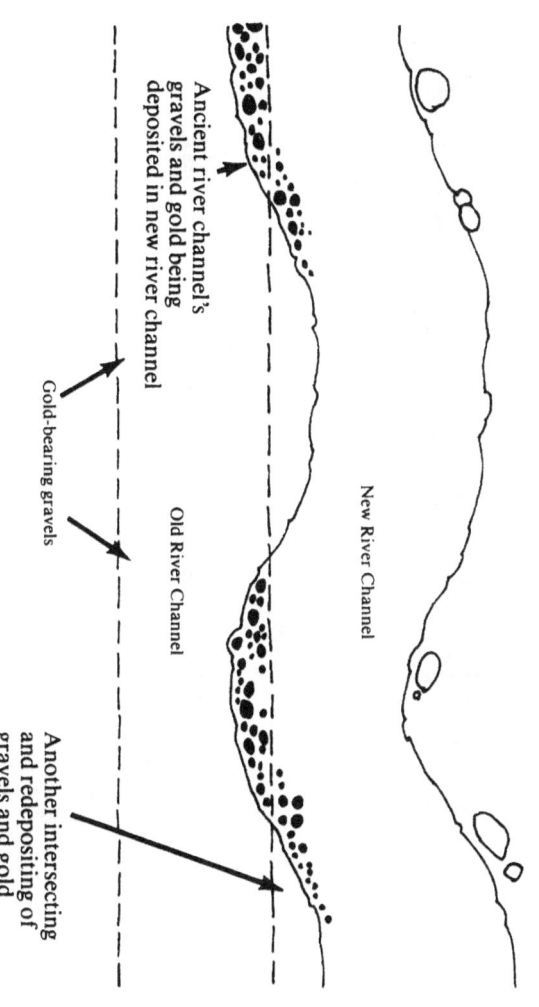

New River Channel

Old River Channel

Ancient river channel's gravels and gold being deposited in new river channel

Gold-bearing gravels

Another intersecting and redepositing of gravels and gold

47

FIGURE 26—MOUNTAIN UPTHRUST

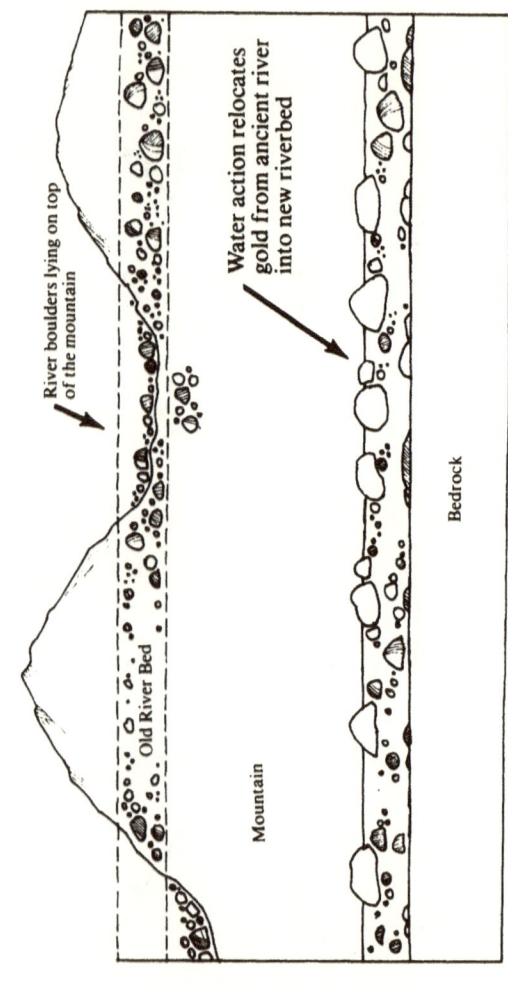

River boulders lying on top of the mountain

Old River Bed

Mountain

Water action relocates gold from ancient river into new riverbed

Bedrock

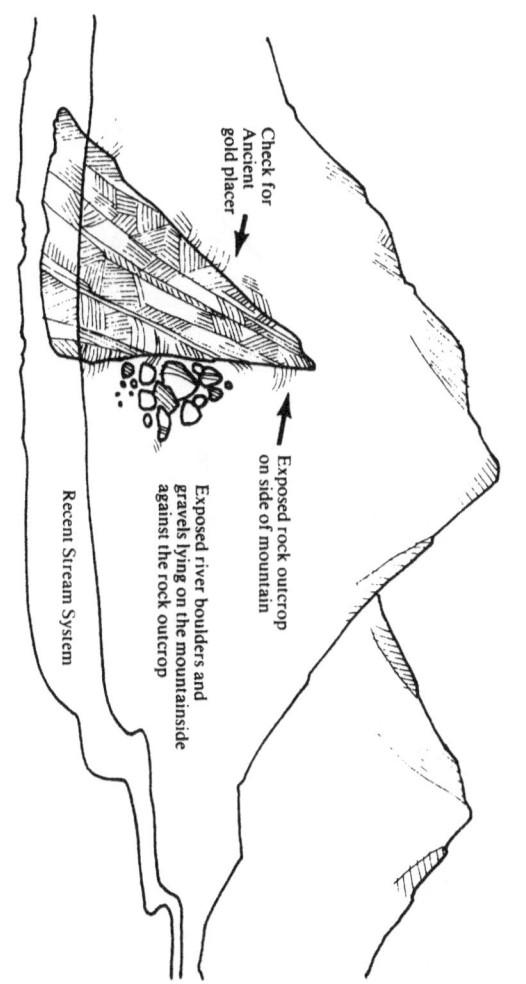

Check for
Ancient
gold placer

Exposed rock outcrop
on side of mountain

Exposed river boulders and
gravels lying on the mountainside
against the rock outcrop

Recent Stream System

FIGURE 27—ANCIENT PLACER

49

FIGURE 28—ANCIENT PLACER

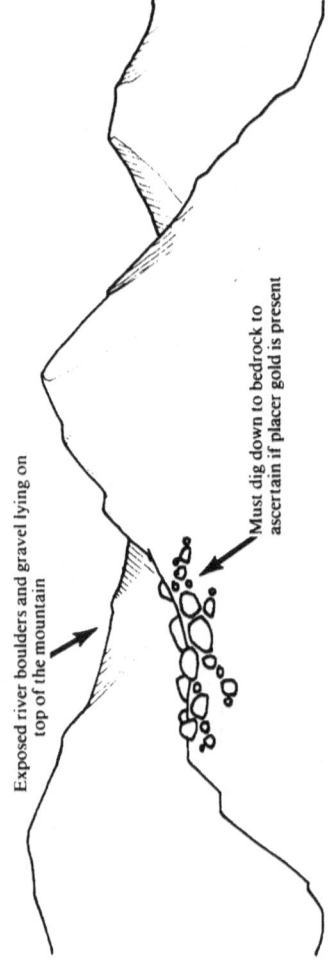

Exposed river boulders and gravel lying on top of the mountain

Must dig down to bedrock to ascertain if placer gold is present

FIGURE 29—GLACIAL MORAINE

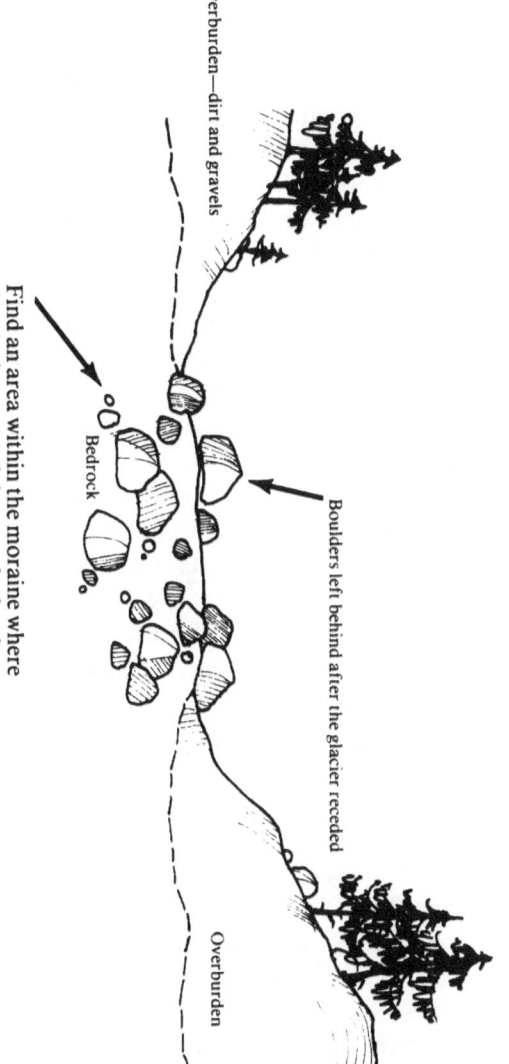

Overburden—dirt and gravels

Find an area within the moraine where the glacier scraped down to bedrock and check for gold placer deposit.

Bedrock

Boulders left behind after the glacier receded

Overburden

have found for finding an ancient placer is by looking for large river boulders and gravels lying on the side of a mountain or, in some instances, on top of the mountain. Once I have located a suspected ancient placer on the side of a mountain, I follow it until I find bedrock, which in the case of Figure 27 is a rock outcrop jutting from the side of the mountain. This outcrop is bedrock, and the ancient stream millions of years ago flowed around it. Climb up to the outcrop and take samples by crevicing—cleaning all the fractures of its material—and work down along the outcrop, searching for other gold traps. I have seen uplifted placers that now lie on the top of a mountain. To work these deposits you must remove the overburden until you reach bedrock and the placer gold that you hope will be there (Fig. 28).

Another origin of gold placer deposits is glacial transportation. Huge glaciers flowed down mountain valleys millions of years ago, ripping lode gold from its host rock and redepositing it in glacial moraines when the Ice Age came to an end. Usually when you spot a glacial moraine, which is easily identifiable by the huge amounts of earth and large boulders left behind, you will see large mounds of earth and huge boulders lying on the valley floor or resting on the side of a hill. As you view the landscape, you will note that no way other than glacial movement could possibly deposit debris of this kind. Within the moraine you could seek out bedrock jutting through the earth to ascertain if gold had been in fact carried within the glacier (Fig. 29). Some substantial finds have been discovered within glacial moraines.

Remember to check all suspected or possible ancient placer deposits, regardless of how far away they may be from the recent stream channel, because gold is where you find it.

Staking Your Claim

If we make a decision based upon the amount of gold that we have taken from our potential gold placer to proceed with further development work, our next step will be to stake, or file, a mining claim. However, if you have only found small amounts of flour gold and no larger gold, you more than likely do not have a gold placer pay streak worth staking. For example, very fine gold, which will pass through a 40 mesh (40 openings per square inch) screen, takes about 40,000 colors to make one ounce of gold. In a situation where you could work a remote gold placer with a small dredge because there is only a few feet of overburden, I still recommend that you claim the site, regardless of its remoteness and ease of mining. On harder-to-mine placers with greater depths of overburden, we definitely would file a claim prior to sampling work because someone could file on our potential placer prior to our completing the sampling and assay phase of development. We already know there is gold in the area because we have found several large flakes and perhaps a few pea-size nuggets and should realize that any type of mining activity will bring other miners into the area. Always secure your potential gold placer by claiming it prior to proceeding with further development work. Later, if sampling and assay results prove that we do not have an economical commercial venture, what is lost—compared to what could be lost if it proved to be a very profitable placer and we find that someone else has filed on it first?

Our first step to filing a mining claim will be to determine exactly where our potential gold placer is located by using a survey map. Then we will tie at least one corner of the placer claim to a section corner, quarter corner, or a township corner of the public land survey, provided that the area has been surveyed. This practice is not required by law, but current regulations do require that the claim or placer must be easily located from written directions (metes and bounds description), usually by using a prominent land feature as a reference point. The BLM land office can tell you if the area has been surveyed and can provide you with a record of the survey at a nominal fee. Also, the National Forest Service that has jurisdiction over the area in which you are mining can supply you with a forest service map showing sections and townships, if they are available. These survey maps will assist you to pinpoint your placer on the map and enable you to tie it to a township corner. Referring your placer's location to a prominent landmark in the immediate area is an excellent idea if the area has not been surveyed and is the smart thing to do even if the area has been surveyed. This is because you might make a mistake in the legal description. If you are having difficulties in ascertaining exactly where your placer is located, the nearest Bureau of Land Management Office or National Forest Service Office can provide you with assistance. Also, they both carry several mining pamphlets that deal with Federal Mining Laws and procedures for staking and filing a claim. The county recorder of the county where your claim is situated could also assist you with your legal description. You may even wish to hire a professional surveyor to assist you. However, with reasonable care and by using a prominent land feature and by tieing its location in with the location of your placer's location you should have no difficulty.

The second step after locating the placer claim is to post a Notice of Location at the discovery site. This will contain the names of the locators, date of location, and the approximate dimensions of the area claimed, plus its geographical location. Printed forms of location notices can be obtained from most print shops. I advise you to place the notice into a glass jar or metal can and to affix it to some permanent object, such as a post or tree, at or very near the discovery site. It is a good idea to have some disinterested party witness the posting and the signing of the notice. Within thirty days after posting the notice of location at the placer claim site you must distinctly mark your placer's boundaries on the ground so that it can be readily traced. You will need a compass when tracing and recording the direction of the boundaries.

To set up the boundaries, I suggest using four fence posts, four by four inches square by four feet six inches in length, set one foot in the ground at each corner of the claim. However, in the case where the stream has a sharp bend in it you may require more than four fence posts in order to follow the curvature of the stream (Fig. 30). The corner posts, whether you are using four or more posts to identify the claim's boundaries, must be marked with the name of the claim; and each post must have a number designation, such as posts one, two, three, and four, and so on, depending on the number of boundary posts being used to adequately mark the boundaries.

Your claim should not exceed 1,500 feet in length along the placer pay streak and shall not extend more than 300 feet on each side of the middle of the placer pay streak. The maximum size, as stated, is 600 feet wide by 1,500 feet long, which is slightly over 20 acres of ground. Later on you may wish to stake additional claims, and that is permissable, provided each additional staked claim has a discovery within the new area being staked. If you wish to form an association of up to eight persons, you are allowed to stake as high as 160 acres in one claim and have only one discovery upon it. For additional information write to your State Bureau of Mines and Geology; they can provide you with a copy of your state's mining laws, which incorporate Federal Mining Laws, and complete data on staking a claim as well as copies of the applicable forms required when staking a claim.

Before setting out the boundary posts, try to determine

FIGURE 30—STAKING A PLACER CLAIM

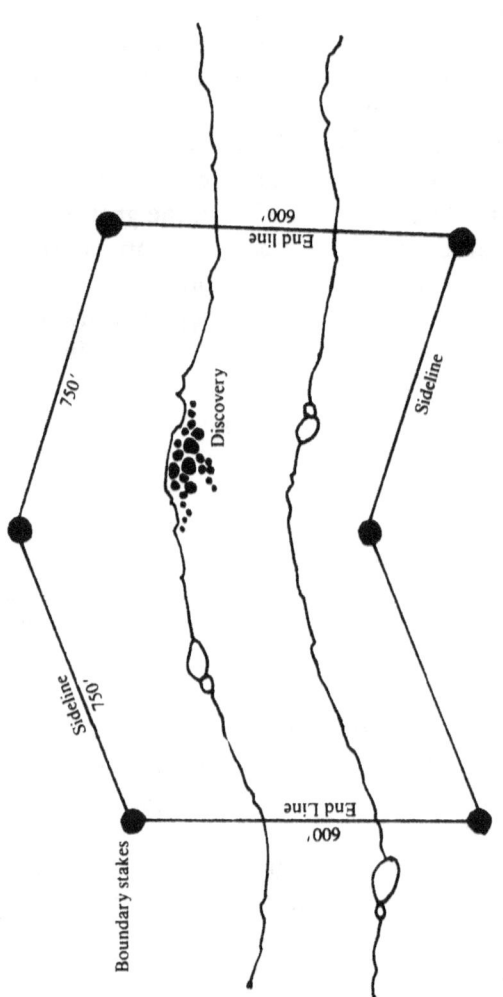

Approximately 20 acres

exactly how the placer gold pay streak runs. Trace it to the best of your ability. After the posting of the Notice of Location at the claim site, you have sixty days in which to do the discovery work to expose your pay streak.

The third step is to record your location by using a Certificate of Location and filing it in the office of the County Clerk of the county in which your placer mining claim is situated. This must be accomplished within sixty days after posting the Notice of Location. In addition, the Federal Land Policy and Management Act of 1976 requires that you must also record your mining claim with the Bureau of Land Management. Their copy of the Certificate of Location must be filed no later than ninety days after the date of posting your Notice of Location. For further information on this act, I urge you to obtain a copy of BLM Circular #2444-A. Both filings may be accomplished after the boundaries are in place. It is necessary to have the Certificate of Location (note that I did not say Notice of Location) notarized before you file it with the County Clerk of the county where the claim is situated and with the Bureau of Land Management. The notary is merely verifying that you are the person who is making the recordation with the County Clerk where the claim is situated and with the Bureau of Land Management. The Certificate of Location can also be obtained from most large print shops and survey stores.

CHAPTER EIGHT

Assaying a Potential Placer

Once you have discovered a potential gold placer, the only way you will know its value is by taking gravel samples and having them assayed for metal content. The assaying of a disseminated gravel gold-bearing deposit is indeed a difficult task because it is very hard to obtain a truly representative sample of the entire deposit. An expeditious assay will save you much exploratory work by letting you know if you should continue with your placer mining operation. When it comes to the sampling and assaying of a placer deposit, I do not recommend that you skimp on costs. Many small miners have been guilty of not performing professional and adequate sampling and assaying methods prior to commencing full-scale mining operations. Consequently they went broke, whereas had they devoted a little more time and money on sampling, they would have known that the gold content per ton of gravels processed would not justify a mining venture. So don't skimp on sampling and assay work, or you, too, may expend unjustified development costs without knowing what you are getting into.

The pitfalls in placer mining are so much greater than those found in hard-rock mining because sampling and assaying is much more difficult within a disseminated deposit. I highly recommend that, if at all possible, you hire a professionally qualified geologist to assist you with your sampling and assay work. If money is a problem, perhaps you can find a geologist that will donate his time for a piece of the action if and when production starts.

58

The most common method of sampling for a placer deposit is by excavating shafts and trenches. These excavations may be made by hand, back hoe, or bulldozer. Sometimes timbering should be used to keep the hole, or trench, from caving in before a sample can be taken. Once your trench is completed, a channel should be cut down the side of the trench approximately twelve inches wide and about six inches deep. A sample should be taken every foot; and because some trenches may be in excess of fifteen feet deep, a large number of samples may be necessary. Also, within the placer deposit area other trenches are made, usually at intervals of fifty to three hundred feet, using a grid system or at sites selected by the geologist based upon geologic features within the area of the placer. Drilling is also a common method for placer deposits. Remember: Don't skimp on sampling costs.

As stated before, larger gold lies on bedrock or within a foot or two above it, and you have to figure if the costs necessary to remove fifteen to twenty feet of overburden will justify the gold value within the whole gravel mass being removed. This is why we must know the approximate gold value within the deposit from the top of the overburden to the larger gold that we hope will be lying on the bedrock.

The names and addresses of reputable assay companies may be obtained through your state's Bureau of Mines. Your state's School of Mines may do your assay work for a nominal fee. Also, you can pick up a copy of several mining publications that are available through larger magazine stores. They contain advertisements of various assay companies showing their services and sometimes their prices.

In 1979, the average recoverable grade of gold mined in placers averaged 0.015 ounce per cubic yard of gravel washed. The tenor, or the gold content, of a deposit varies with the price of the metal; the higher the price of gold, the lower the metal content necessary to make it profitable. With the higher price of gold now, many claims that were unprofitable will once again be profitable. However, in any hard rock ore deposit or disseminated placer deposit, the value of the recoverable gold within the deposit must be greater than the cost of its extraction. Profit depends upon the amount of recoverable gold and other metals within the deposit; the price of those metals; and the cost of mining, treating, transporting, and marketing. I believe that access to the placer deposit is the most important single factor. Can you get your mining equipment in and out of the area to be mined without costly construction? Mining costs, such as having to build a road or having to fly equipment into the placer site, can make a fairly rich placer deposit uneconomical.

CHAPTER NINE

Whether to Sell or to Operate Your Claim

If you find that you have a good producing placer, you will have to decide whether to operate it on your own, form a partnership, or sell it to a small mining operator. Normally, a large mining company would not be interested in a placer deposit. They are more interested in lode claims containing large ore reserves. If you find a small mine operator willing to work your claim, he will generally agree only to give you a percentage of the gold recovered. If he thinks you have an extremely good claim, he may pay a minimum royalty annually. I know of one lease agreement where the operator or mining company agreed to a royalty of 8 percent net smelter returns. Also, when you lease your claim, insist that a minimum number of dollars of work is done on the property annually. Before negotiating any type of agreement, consult with an attorney who has expertise in the mining field.

If you decide to operate your placer claim on your own, I am certain that a good assay report and a favorable report from your geologist will find you an investor for your placer mining venture. Whatever you decide, be sure that you have a signed and notarized agreement between the company or other person and yourself. And be sure to remain in the operation so that you know what is going on. Nuggets have a habit of disappearing when the venture is not being overseen by you or a trusted representative.

GOOD PROSPECTING

www.ingramcontent.com/pod-product-compliance
Lightning Source LLC
Chambersburg PA
CBHW021239280526
45784CB00005B/2155